Compass of My Thoughts

Reflections by a child

Aditri Gaonkar

BookLeaf Publishing
India | USA | UK

Made with ❤ on the BookLeaf Publishing Platform
www.bookleafpub.in
www.bookleafpub.com

Dedication

To my family and friends for always being there for me.

Acknowledgement

Firstly, I would like to thank my parents and grandparents for their dedication and support throughout my writing journey, this book is largely inspired by such values. Constantly, I have learnt valuable life lessons and experiences through my friends, family and peers. Wholeheartedly, I thank the BookLeaf publishing team for making this book possible. Thank you so much everyone.

Preface

Through observations and reflections, we gain a deeper understanding of ourselves and these attributes contribute to who we are as a person and society as a whole. These next few pages explore poetry through unique angles, where thoughts and ideas are immersed in a world and craft of words. Poetry dives into complex, valuable emotions and lessons that collectively, as a community are important to learn. As you journey through this book, you will be immersed in the importance of self development, and being your personal best.

Stepping Stones

Potential that ripples through
Possibilities of our power of thought
Infinite concepts hidden, vast
Shifting our futures everyday

The interconnections between all
Every thought, could shape your life
Perspectives of our mindsets
To be constructive through actions

Seemingly insignificant insights
Have the might to change the way we think
A philosophical approach
Reflect on those effects

Trails of moments yet to be
Every thought imperative
To the making of our universe
Understanding that small changes are pivotal

Cultivate lines of thinking that challenge
That inspire and motivate
Opportunities over obstacles
Make a difference.

Dance of Opposites

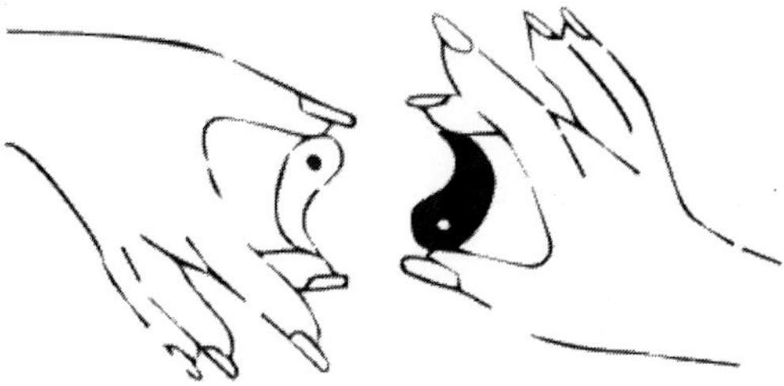

Life, a rich dance , so true
Of opposites in embrace
A paradox that carries us on
In spirit, an endless flame

For we need both joy and sorrow
Certainty and doubt
We can feel the contrary
Of our states of mind

A fragile line we go in and out of
We cannot continue on it
Oh, the vibrancy of existence
The multitudes of being a human

In moments of simplicity,
The most complex findings arise
Collapsing into simple cores of connection
The vitality we exude.

Hand in hand, what truly means
Our existence's journey
Dread and bliss, quite the enigma
In Contradictions, we find the best

Lost in the glitch

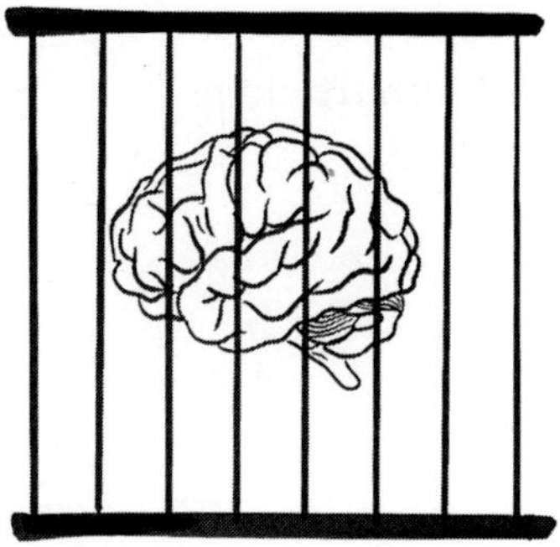

FOMO, a process of dread
The constant pressure pushing against you
A buzzing hum pulls me in
To miss out, I drown in my scrolling

Chasing moments I long to be in
Missing out on those memories I could have made
As their thrill echoes through the screen
Signifying I'm lost in their glow

But that rush, the chaos
Do I need it, now?
Of peaceful ambiance
What is really needed

A break, a little rest
Not lonely, but to recharge
To grasp harmony within
Turn FOMO into freedom.

Real Riches

Don't seek the prize of glory
Or validation from others
Basing your worth on their praise
Leads to only self destruction

Our true essence is buried in our souls
Of chasing curiosity sincerely
When it guides us as our compass
We break from the abyss of their approval

Limits, we break free from
Untamed souls seek their own paths
So pure, the truth we have
Curiosity, a journey of life

Let your heart seek the unknown
Not for them but for you
A path of knowledge for you alone
For wonders, real riches

Writing On...

Not every chapter ends quite the same
A myth reciting stories of closure at the end
Some paths wonder to unknown destinations
A continuous story where chapters don't need to end

Finding peace in the unpredictable
And in the lessons yet to learn
Beyond the stereotypical fairytale endings
We know of a greater sense

Letting go of the need of ending one to start one
For moving on doesn't have to be from an end
We choose to transcend at any moment
Perhaps to roads leading to each other again

Imperfection leads to the best results
Definitive endings are of the past
Concrete understandings , not needed
To find letting go of the deep desire.

Where real experiences showcase their value
To trust in the unresolved
For the world we shape keeps moving
And we are Adapting and Aligning

Quiet Defiance

Bold steps which leave a trace
Not necessarily a bold display
A whisper of different ways
Navigating this maze

Defying norms, breaking free
Quiet courage holds the key
A hidden spark, true to me
Choosing my way to be

Chasing the pulse of contradiction
Where we speak of our affirmations
Speaking lines of these convictions
Our ways, a great expedition

The little ways, fierce and formidable
Together, the will is indomitable
Collective spirits, indefatigable
The depth of a force undeniable

Not in loud words, but actions that count
For true freedom, a peak we mount
People's worth not in the world's account
Silence over noise surmounts .

My fire

The inner unbound ignition
Clues of fulfilment we gather
Purpose in our passion
Channeling it productively

Breathing life into shaping your map
Don't dim your fire, but let it blaze
By not suppressing the kindle
Not fleeting distractions, but visceral desires

My soul's spreading wildfire,
The reflection of my heart
A curious light at the end of the tunnel
A symphony I compose

A burning passion in my core
My guiding compass
A relentless drive for purpose
Bringing clarity to me.

Mirrors

A whisper within, in their thoughts
Reflect on deeper truths
Each person a mirror to what we've been
taught
Befriending ourselves within

From the flaws sought and lessons learnt
The inside of our lives
To what we know and yearn
Finding pieces of our selves

Like a puzzle, they fit together
A time to know through them
Would I have stuck by forever
Or pushed away with disdain

We look to what they may wonder
In every interaction so significant
Embrace every person, a time to ponder
In who we are and can be

Toxic Positivity

"Good Vibes only!" They always say,
Keeping feelings hidden away.
Toxic mindsets, lurking inside
Where sorrow never felt divine

Still, those thoughts speak of truth
Only to be pushed down, a stern reproof
"The oh so great bright side" hiding dark
secrets
To mask our souls, from any regrets

This is not healthy, to hide who we are!
They say we are not up to par
For being human, is not always whole
To be entrapped in their control

We aren't perfect, and that's okay!
Never should we keep emotions at bay!
Express yourself and let the inner-self shine
After all, my emotions are mine

Intercultural Awareness

The sounds of our cultures
Of ancient scriptures
Each day, a new venture
Of past, present and future.

I ask myself 'who am I'
To guide myself through my flight
Of life's great journeys and how they shine
And what more I will go on to find

A universal way of to be
To explore and be free
Cultures, tradition and all I will see
Mixing together in all sorts of glee

To learn more about each other
To unite, and share together,
Deepening understandings even further
Awareness about one another

Keeping who we are, along
Intercultural relations, always strong
Walk with hope, and sing our song
Moving forward, where we belong.

Productivity over "busy"

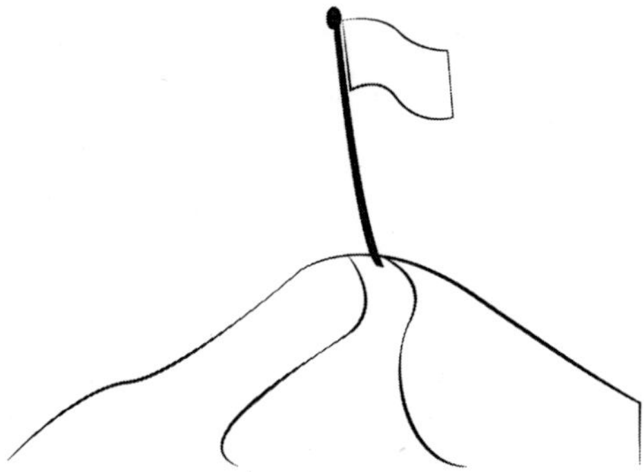

Cluttered tasks of here and there
Meetings, calls of every hour
Chaotic schedules never seeming to end
Chasing the promotions to power

Yet, our mindsets still believe
Success rides on frantic pace
We move toward which goal?
No time for joy's embrace

Shift the gears, to productivity
Set goals that YOU want to reach
How much more to suffer in prices of haste?
Where beyond there is much much more to
teach

Productive over busy
Finding ways to restore energy and goals
Organisation, a vital tool
That is an essential role.

A Fleeting Gift

Time, the most precious of all,
A fleeting gift, that slips away
It's more than we may see.
A one time chance

Every second, we deeply claim
The moments where we learn the most.
A diamond of time, lost once gone
Never to be found again

More time cannot be made
So, feel every second that passes
The heartbeat of true value
A silent gold worth much more

A single day, a great fortune to be found
Never to be taken advantage of
Devoting it to the greatest purposes
It's stories untold, yet vesting in power

To act fast, to catch it
To understand the true meanings
To discover what we learn
Time, the most valuable of all.

Let your words flow

To regret, is to miss
To wish that the truths were spoken
Of the lies inside, to let the truth unleash
All we withheld from within

The words we needed to let flow
Embrace the chances, of dreams in our hearts
The chapter left blank in our own books
An empty string of our thoughts

At the end, it's not about what we missed
How we should have done it
But, to find a way to write those pages
Pages in our books of life

What we hold back, never to be shared
Keeping it unsaid; it's forever undone
The time is now, to share your stories
To find your words and let them shine.

Energies of Us

Personality, ingrained in us, deep
A hushed look through other people's eyes
Energy that flows through our souls
Sewn through us.

A quiet force we live by
What we give, what we give
Of ourselves and more
Unknowingly, making us whole

Leave a trace of our thoughts
A current which flows through our souls
Words we share, a free mind
Moments in which we pause

A subconscious feeling of life
Of how we perceive
Of what's unfurled, what unbound
A quiet, unvoiced grace

The Meaning Of Life

Beyond the horizon,
a discovery of perspective blooms.
For the tender lagoon,
Of life and zen's mystery.

It blooms throughout
For we need to grow it
The essence of solace
And deep reverie

Radiances of serenity
Only we can find
Our 'meaning of life'
Whispers only we understand

Perspective rules it all!
See through different scenarios
And find the true meanings
For you.

Start Again

Shared communities, unite and arise,
A new beginning,
A time that is bright
Showering us with vibrant futures
New dreams to chase, a new flight

A time to reflect, present and past,
To look to the future, bring hope to all.
A New year, an impact of new discovery,
As the old year we had, comes to a fall.

Voyages of beyond, to persevere,
The zen of a new start, not always so clear.
Many horizons of possibilities, a vibrant
onset,
Aspirations take us through, not to fear.

A challenge of wonder, finding a start,
Perspectives of a new year, a shared thought.
Start new habits, to begin,
All the fun the year before had brought.

Making it count, what really matters
A time to celebrate, to find anew,
Happy new year, for all to share.
To leave one and find one, to be brand new...

Blooms Of Patience

Oh, the flow of understanding
With timings of fate
An individual pace each day.
A bloom into a new wait

A tender hush, of calm within
Which grows through every test
Learn to have no rush or strain
Balances in our lives

Choose to wait, restrain demands
Be at peace with the process
To build on this journey
Unfolding a gentle time

Just be there.
For the greats, knew when to pause
To let the world flow
Tranquility through the soul.

Attend to this strength
Not a weakness but a power
Of knowing things will come, when it's time
For now, Patience...

Purpose

To work toward our dreams
Moving forward with every day,
They don't owe us, we owe ourselves
As we shape our chosen places

Move with life's purpose toward
A secret which lies within
Create, shift, change
Where we will be

A force, untamed, we have to find
What we seek, in our eyes
In what we reap, what we sow
For opportunities slip away

Endlessly, at times we wish,
We took
Our desires, try to grasp
A feel of entitlement to each time
Makes greed overtake

To be the sketch, to paint the future
To take hold of what we have
To know the next steps toward
Because it is in our hands.

We are Shrines

What our souls try to hide
Of an ache our body has to pay
Our body shows from every side
Burdens of burnout

Chaos takes over, an unending struggle
Between thoughts weighing us down
Our temple of a body has to juggle
Pleas of needs and rest

Find the light to lift us above
Care, and peace will follow
An awareness we acknowledge and love
In the body's everlasting flow

A time to prevent it before it's too late
You aren't alone, we can wake
To times of self care these days
Holding the truth in our mental seas

For deep within, we need a break—
To find those balances in-between
For our body and soul's sake
We need to listen deeply.

Building Blocks

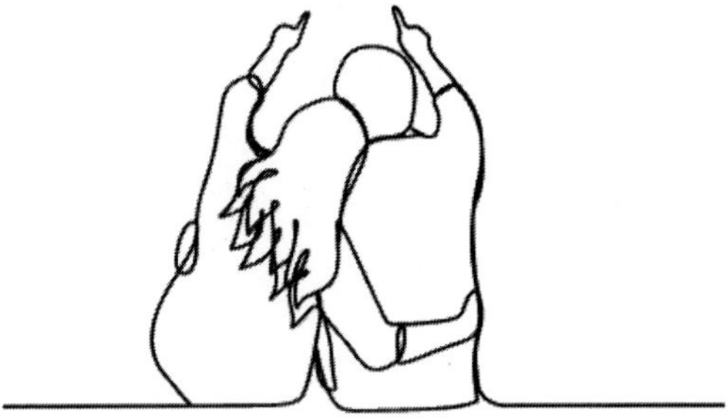

Spoken love of the heart.
Of what could be, not what is.
A rise of our faith in others.
Seeds to sprout, a new dawn

Large dreams to achieve
Goals yet we have to unwrap
Building on the future
Of skies anew

The potential of a bright future
That we cohesively can make
Plan and dream
The course ahead

A building block of their journeys,
To support and see what will be
Don't judge actions, rather guide
A map of directions and paths

Connections from Within

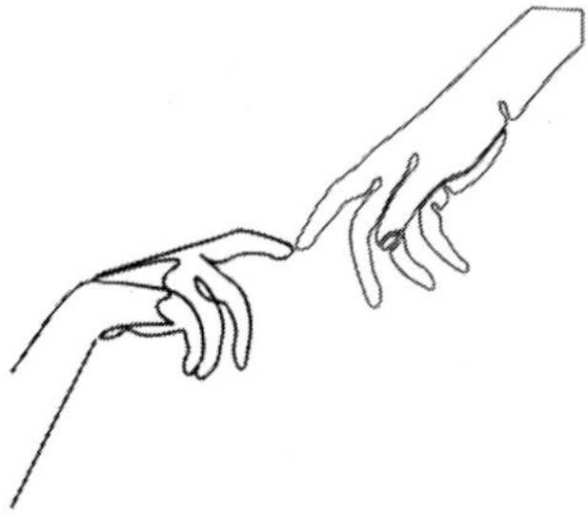

Forged bonds of trust
A rhythm we create
A free heart, open and pure
Not to those always sure.

To trust the path we take
Take your time, gently, free
No grants, no swift returns
Forged in a stillness

Truly deeply rooted,
Not a race, but something more
Connect, in moments fleeting
How a bond so pure lasts

No promises to abide
But a gentle spark we see
Meaningful, with grace
Not in instant gratification

To let go, to find
The right times for you
The true meanings
Of connections true.

Breaking Free

A journey which is blocked,
Stopping the growth unfolding,
Clutching the path with our own hands,
Fear of it slipping away

Trusting the road, which we build
'How' we should,
set limits on our ability,
Hoax maps , set paths
For life's truth, yet be told

A certain way, we must
Beyond the clouds, much more we find
A journey's not in what we read
But rather what we will go on to write

Craving the answers, we need now
An unanswered question, lingering
But we have the answers, in our minds
To change from 'limits' to 'discoveries'

Masks over reality

Truth can be ugly
Seeking sugar coated lies
Is our solution

A deep illusion
A mask in reality
Self deception, repressed facts

We don't have to hide,
To face it, is true courage
Power to set us free

Oh, contradiction
Dismantle "safe" fantasies
We run and deny

We can't always run
So when you face truth head on
No filter. No lies.

Leading to progress
Reveal yourself the real you now
Heal toward the truth.

Subconscious Sprouts

Subconscious corners of our thoughts,
Fresh perspective sprouts
Breakthroughs in a fresh awakening
Of deliberate pauses.

Giving ourselves spaces to "unfocus"
To dwell in our tangled minds
Draws the soul into a suffocating coil
Of a cage where we wither

Allowing our brains to breathe
To unfurl in a salutary calm
Equanimity, steers us through
Loosening grips on urge for control

Burnout, what we may succumb to
In repose, to wander through our thoughts
To soar with new wings of being free
Composure in the stillness.

The Time is Now

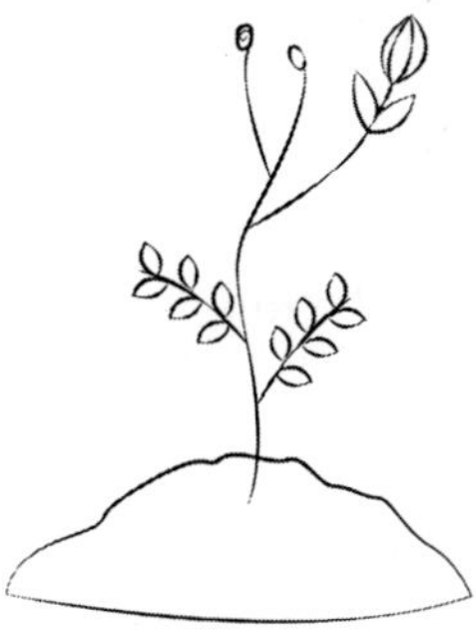

A seed changed my life.
A seed which wanted to be,
To be something great.

Hello seed, I say.
It grumbles and looks away.
What's wrong? I ask.

That tree, it's so wise!
Everyone around respects it.
Not me, just a seed...

Why can't I grow now?
Then I will be like the tree—
Always with esteem.

Oh seed, why oh why,
you want to grow up so soon?
One day you will, seed!

Enjoy now, you know!
Seed-life will not be long.
Don't be in a rush.

Soon all will want you—
To meet you and your wisdom!
No relaxation!

Growing up is hard.
Many problems you don't know!
Be in the moment.

Do you want to rush?
Not live life to the fullest?
Seed, your time is now!

Why compare always, seed?
Big trees have lots of problems!
Wishing their youth back.

The seed stops and thinks.
It stares at the wise, smart tree.
I know, says the seed.

The problems and all.
Alas no one respects me!
See, they pick on me!
Because I'm so small.
Everyone thinks I can't do great things.
Size is my drawback...

That's why I hurry!
To prove them wrong someday soon.
Then, I'll show them all!

Size doesn't matter!
Why can't you do great things now?
No need to wait, seed!

For your size is great!
Youth is your advantage, seed.
Prove all of them wrong!

For your size is great!
Youth is your advantage, seed.
Prove all of them wrong!
We stare at the sky.

And as the horizon sets,
Yes, says the seed
You are so, so right!
I will do something great!
Yes, the time is now.

Nurture Our Future

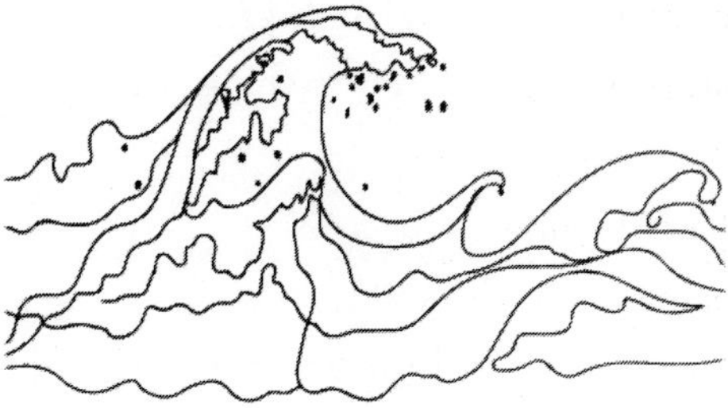

In the oceans symphony,
Melodies play deep below
Sprinkled with wonders of mystery,
Coral's colorful tapestry grows.

Like a spider weaving its web,
Nature crafts a net of life
As I stand at the ebb,
I admire its beauty, so rife.

Albeit all this splendor,
A tragic tale lies in our fate.
Without any defenders,
Prisons of plastic search for inmates.

Our once majestic waters,
Die before our own eyes.
Will you ignore this slaughter?
Hear their pleas , listen to their cries!

How do we help, you say?
Remember the three R's.
Reduce, Reuse, and Recycle this way,
Come on, let's play our part!

It's up to us , the guardians,
To unite and pledge its safety,
As we stand in the hues of the horizon,
I believe we can preserve this beauty...

Together, We Shine

Like fireflies dancing through a dark meadow,
Stars twinkle in the vast expanse,
All so radiant and bright,
Its effect takes us into a trance.

My eyes fix on a group of ethereal orbs,
Their radiance steals the show.
A jewel as ancient as time,
Making my heart glow.

Huddled together like angels looking down at us,
I begin to join the dots,
More magnificent than I could ever imagine,
It makes sense now, all their plots

As they weave together, no one can deny,
Their teamwork as one whole,
Painting the sky with ancient tales,
Creating a story, a cosmic scroll.

Portraying a mural of grace and beauty,
Their teamwork guides us through the night,
A constellation—
pure and elegant
Together as one, their unity taking flight.

Like a grand parade in the velvet sky,
They dance as not one but something more,
Twirling through lifetimes of old and new,
Many galaxies yet to explore.

Let their example lead for us,
As each one plays their part,
Guiding each other through the makings,
Of a new constellation, united full of heart.

Be The Light

In the depths of the night, one thing still
glows,
As the blanket of night begins to grow.
Its light, a loyal friend that's always there,
The illuminating light of gleams and glares.

Guiding us through the darkest days,
Where shadows stretch, dance and sway,
A sentinel stands proud and tall,
A streetlight, warm and steady when twilight
falls.

The night's stable, silent trait,
A maker of all the greats.
It's not just a streetlight, no it's something
more,
Bringing peace to the night, letting dreams
soar.

Such a simple thing, yet on it we rely,
However it is always ever nigh,
Making sure, the roads are clear,
A beacon of safety always near,

Let's all be like this simple light,
Making each other's path so bright.
Simple yet extraordinary, taming shadows
and the gloom,
While the glow, softly blooms.

Ignite Your Way

I know that every single one of you,
Who is reading this,
Has been challenged at something.
Probably challenged at multiple things.

You've probably also tried it,
So many times,
That you just want,
To give up.

But is that the key?
Trying and if you fail,
You just stop it all.
Because you were challenged?

But I will let you,
In on a secret,
It's ok to fail!
I know you have probably heard it too many times.

Don't give up,
You can do this.
One day it will pay off,
Keep doing it.

Because the more you do,
You ignite the spark
Of curiosity,
Let that spark be a flame.

Soon it will be a fire,
And the more you keep trying.
One day you will become,
The match.

I wish...

I wish I was tall like them.
I wish I was smart like them.
I wish I was sporty like them.
I wish I was musically talented like them.
I wish I was more attractive like them.
I wish I was good at that like them.
I wish I was funny like them.
I wish I was exactly like them!
Some days I think I want to be like them,
Not just like them,
But exactly like them.
I wish, I wish, I wish, I was them.
Many people think this every day.
But they don't realise,
That they are unique.

That they are themselves.
Because the truth is,
You are never them.
You are You,
And you are amazing.
Only you have a fingerprint just like yours,
Only you have talents that make you unique.
Even twins can never be the same.
No one is!
Being confident is not saying,
"They will like me".
Instead it is saying,
" I don't care what they think".
So embrace what makes you truly you,
And don't want something others have.
Because when you find the diamond in yourself,
No one can stop you.

Grandmother's Love

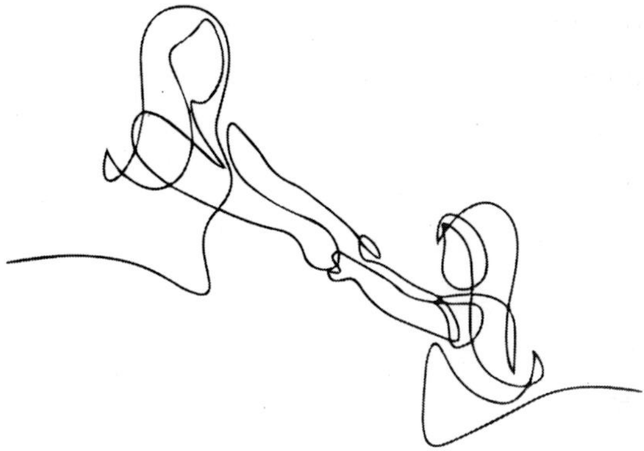

Cuddled in her warm embrace,
The one who is always near.
Whose heart is as rich as gold,
In mine, I hold her dear.

She feeds you with treats,
Filled with care and love,
So graceful and sweet,
Like a peaceful dove.

Her love, like no other,
Like candy with endless sugar.
Patient and calm,
And sparks of joy she triggers.

She puts you to sleep,
Quiet as a mouse.
I love her so much,
Who brings delight in the house.

So underestimated,
Who plays a big role!
I love you grandmother,
In my heart, you're gold.

True Happiness

There was once an old man,
With his grandkids.
One night as they slept,

For bedtime,
The children wanted a story,
“Tell us!” they would shout.

“Ok!” The grandfather would reply,
” I’ll tell you a story that is real, and about me.”
And so he began,

Painting his stories in his imagination.
As the kids leaned in,
To listen closer.

"I was a very good artist,
I thought that one day I would sell,
Many paintings that I had made,

And become a famous painter"
"When it came to university selections,
I wanted to apply for an art school,

But all my peers took another field,
Everyone told me I should too!"
"That I'll end up starving as an artist,

That it is not reliable,
I would never make it,
And regret it lifelong,"

"Peer pressure weighed me down,
One by one by one,
It seemed like the best choice at the time,

So I applied for another field."
"Throughout my working days,
I hated the job!

Never made me happy,
As much as painting did."
"I feel like so much more,

Could have been accomplished.
If I had just followed my dreams,
And did what I wanted to."

"Alas I did not,
And here I am,
Forever regretting,

That choice."
The kids showed misery in their faces
And slowly one of them said,

"You should have done what made you happy,
What truly made you happy!
"Such wise words,"

The grandfather replied
"I do regret it,
But it's too late!"

"It's never too late,
You can still do it,
And you can do,

What made you feel joy!"
The grandfathers thinks,
About the child's words,

And did something,
That made him happy.
He went on to sell many,

Successful paintings,
And always took pride,
In what made him truly happy.

Don't Fall Prey

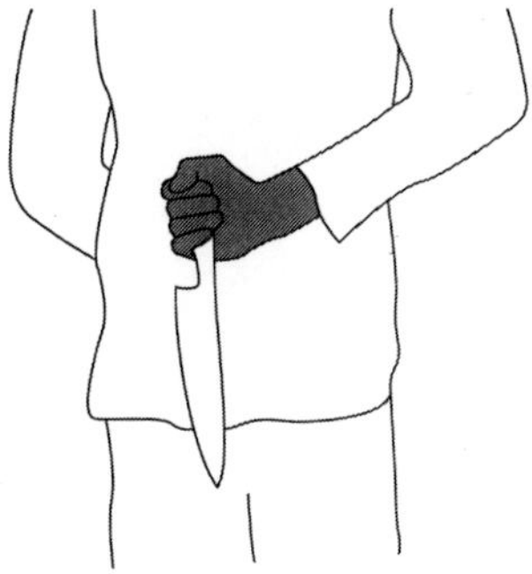

In the branches up high,
A bird perched to rest,
In the blue azure sky,
With its vivid crest.

It did not know,
What the shadows hid.
Of deception, a soon foe,
Under the forest's dense lid.

A dark personality,
To pounce upon a chance.
After watching his prey,
The thirst of his quick glance.

"Come down little bird.
Let's become friends,
I'll give my word !"
Little did she know it was all just pretend!

Not seeing his deception,
Her heart, full of trust,
A simple perception,
Thinking it was a must.

As soon as she landed,
To the horror of all!
She was left stranded,
But no one heard the bird's call.

The snake slithered high and low,
Desperate to catch his victim.
In a burst of wings, she left her predator far below,
As she nearly fell prey to the snake's cunning system.

Be Humble.

In the animal kingdom,
Many gathered around,
To listen to the tiger's tales.
Of his glory and pleasure,

And his tales of him are so great.
And how he was the best of all.
Many animals got fed up,
And stopped listening.

To the tigers wayward chants.
They all knew his lies,
And how he boasted about his fame.
And wealth that he acquired.

One day he told a story of how,
He won a medal in running.
And no one else could beat him.
"I'm certainly the best of all,

No one as fast as me,
Who ever tries, will break their ego!"
"Why don't we have a running race,
And see who is really the fastest?"

Suggested the Cheetah.
So came the day of the race,
All animals lined up,
Ready to break the tiger's ego.

Ready, set, go! the horn blared.
The race had started.
The elephant and cheetah, in the lead,
The tiger is far behind.

He came last in the race.
And bowed to his shame.
You shouldn't boast,
As it makes others think you are ignorant...

And everyone will know you're a liar.
So the tiger vowed,
Never to boast again.
And always remain humble.

Mother's Love

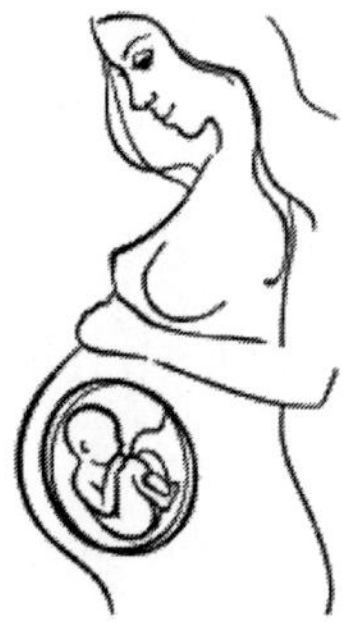

As dawn breaks, and the morning light spills,
On the branches I see,
A woven nest made out of love,
Where the mother bird spreads her wings so
free.

Tiny ones in their mother's embrace,
Forever protected with the warmth of safety.
A mother's duty, never done,
As she goes off to her tasks daily.

She hovers in the air, off to find food,
For her little ones need it soon,
With everything that she does,
Mothers are our boon!

After she returns, it is lesson time,
The biggest part of a bird's life,
She knows it's time for skies, to view,
The wind serenades their journey with its distant fife.

"Feel the breeze and keep relaxed,
Embrace the air with heart.
For it is time for the journey,
To make your mark."

Leaping off the branches, with several tries,
The mother encourages them more.
And even though they think they can't,
A mother always knows in her core.

After multiple tries of failure and setbacks,
Their wings flap midway through their leap.
As they hover in the sky and glide through the air,
She'd known they'd rise and never weep.

The journey into life had just begun,
With their mother by their side.
And as they flew through clouds and sky,
They knew their mother was their guide.

A Mosquito's Courage

Ever thought about,
A mosquito's courage?
Why, it is so brave.

Though it's tiny in size,
Can get squashed so very soon,
It always attacks.

It has one purpose,
Won't stop until it gets it.
It is always there.

Quite ironic, right?
You might think that it isn't .
But would YOU risk it?

Just to reach your goal,
Would YOU be ready for risk?
Probably not, right?

I think it is time,
To acknowledge this small one.
A mosquito's courage.

Fly Higher

Where the wind pirouettes, and clouds sway
and drift,
A kite flies high above.
Its secure string holding it up,
With care, patience and love.

It floats through the air like a magnificent
dove,
Only with the support of a string.
Ascending through the air with colors bright,
Like a cheerful melody to sing.

But if that string is cut or frayed,
Then mayhem will be set free.
Or if the wind changes direction,
It will seek its liberty.

Everything around the kite,
Changes how it soars,
Just one thing that is wrong,
Could shake it to its core.

Everything around the kite,
Changes how it flies.
So cut off all the bad,
And take flight in the skies.

Do not surround yourself,
With people who wish you the worst.
Or else it will be a struggle,
Hard for you to reverse.

Positivity does the trick,
Cut yourself off from toxic peers!
Then you can soar high above,
And explore your potential's frontiers!

Grandfather's Love

The one who works tirelessly,
Just for us.
His strength, an iron,
Which never rusts.

Whose wisdom shows us,
Life's many paths.
His love is a constant,
Full of heart.

He makes you smile,
Even after a long day.
Guides you through the tough,
And shows you the way.

He does all he can,
He knows if you're sad.
He who makes everything better,
To have him, I'm so glad!

So Grandpa, you know,
That you mean so much to me!
I can always see the depth,
Of his love for me.

Gratefulness Goes A Long Way

In the heart of the jungle,
With dense biodiverse species,
Lay the majestic Lion,
As he watched over his kingdom.

While up high above,
Through the cobalt sky,
Flew the butterfly,
With her colors shining like a kaleidoscope.

Both came to a rest,
Down below.
But with very different mindsets,
Of their lives.

Ahh what a great day! Full of air and joy!
Thank you universe!
You are really so great!
Thanks for everything!

The butterfly went on praising,
And thanks
For everything,
With a full heart.

The lion simply laughed,
Oh what are you thanking for?
You were chased by many animals!
Yet are so happy?

You should not thank,
As so many problems come in your life,
Yet you are foolish,
And thank everyone for your problems,

Oh Lion, I may have problems in my life,
But I also have happiness.
Why highlight the bad?
When I can focus on the good!

Not everyone is as fortunate as us sometimes!
So why shall I say my problems are worse?
Everyone has problems,
But what will I get by being sad and unhappy?

The lion thinks about this for a while,
And understands that there are many
problems in his life.
But also good things that are often not
thought of!
So why highlight the bad?

Balance of Life

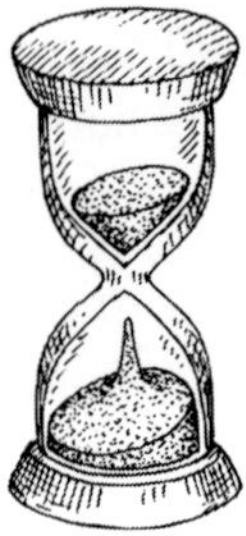

Have you ever heard the saying,
"Time and tide waits for no one."
Everyone says I'll do it later.

But when it comes to the deadline,
We all frantically panic.
To finish assignments, work and important deadlines.

In everyone's busy schedules,
These days we have no time.
And are often stressed.

We don't have time for breaks,
Or anything else.
24/7 it is work.

So the first priority is work.
Then leisure.
But keep taking breaks!

You shouldn't delay things,
But you should also take time to relax,
So find your balance!

Interconnected

The connection of a human brain,
One to another,
Is actually quite complicated.

Friendships, relationships and family—
All connected.
It's the time we spend,

With each other.
When we bond,
We create different pathways of life.

We lean into each other.
When sad, happy or just in the moment.
We're always there.

So get out there.
Create new ways,
Of relationships.

Because we are all connected to one another,
I guess you could say,
We are all interconnected.

Father's Love

The one who is ambitious,
And works toward his dreams.
Full of empathy,
A guiding gleam.

His strength and hope,
Lifts us all.
Helping us up,
When we fall.

Protective as a shield,
And cares with love.
He lifts us,
Up above.

Motivated and driven,
He guides us through.
He's always there,
Forever true!

Plastic's Plight

You have probably seen protests,
Against overusing plastic,
And polluting our oceans and seas.
How plastic kills our environment,

And marine life caught in the traps.
Unable to break free.
But have you ever thought,
From a plastic's point of view?

Just dumped into the ocean floor.
How it is never used properly
Without care or moderation.
Humanity just ignores it.

Bag by bag littered around.
How it feels like,
Such a waste.
Never cared for,

Or used properly.
And when discarded, carelessly placed.
So let's take the effort,
To care for the plastic.

And our one planet—
After all moderation,
Is the key.
And this earth is our garnet!

Expect Nothing

In the mornings, fresh awaken,
As the sun begins to rise.
The hive gets ready for the bloom,
Of flowers and their prize.

The buzzing of bees,
Surround the sky.
As to collect nectar,
From the flowers nearby.

They go off to their journey,
To find treasure for the hive,
As they dance around,
The flowers are thriving.

The flower does not expect,
Anything in return.
Simply it gives its nectar,
Without anything to earn.

See, if we always expect,
Something to receive.
Then greed might become a habit,
Then only ourselves that we deceive.

So let's take the time,
In gratitude and giving.
So what we receive,
Is the heart that we're bringing.

Hard Work

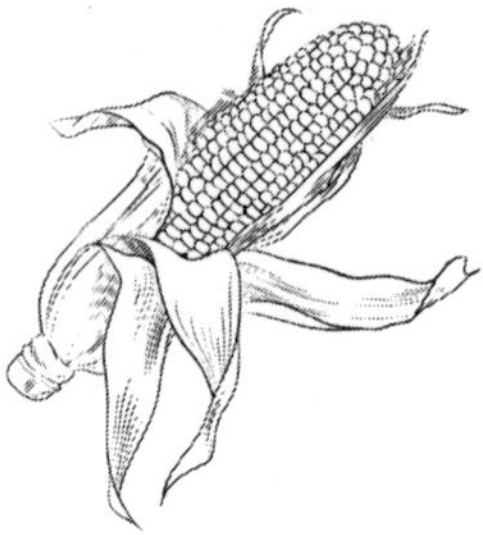

Underneath the summer breeze,
An ant toils away with quiet peace
Through twilight's fall and dawn's hues,
Picking grain, by grain to later use.

He believes his work will soon pay off,
While all the other animals laugh and scoff.
Yet he persists to reach his goal,
And endures the pain and the toll.

What a funny animal, who thinks he's so
smart!
They tease and mock him at his start.
I will show them, he says with grit!
He darts through the field and just won't
quit.

Eventually, the other animals soon depart.
As they have to play their own part.
The winter is coming, and they need to
prepare.
As food and water will quickly be scarce!

Throughout the long winter days,
The hard work soon paid off.
But all the other animals who jeered at his
size,
Soon realised his brain and might.

You see, the ant had large stocks of food,
As he worked hard with a determined mood.
While all the others who jeered and jested,
Had run out of food, with less and less.

But the ant had plenty and shared with care,
All others were grateful beyond comparison.
They realised that hard work is not something
to forget,
And a purpose in the goals we set.